TALES OF THE OLD HIGH

THE PARISH CHURCH OF INVERNESS THROUGH THE AGES

BY ROSS MARTIN

ISBN 978-0-9926198-0-0

Text and Photographs © Ross Martin 2013

Published by Old High St. Stephen's Church of Scotland 2013

Revised and updated 2017

Printed by A4 Design and Print Ltd, Inverness

PREFACE

We've often urged Ross Martin, our resident historian, to put into print his many tales of the Old High. Now he has done so, in this delightfully quirky volume. It will stand as fitting companion to the history of the Old High by the Rev FJL MacLauchlan, and the Centenary History of St Stephen's by the late Malcolm Cumming. But it will make fascinating reading, not just for those interested in Church History, but for anyone with an interest in the history of Inverness and the Highlands.

Out of ancient charters, Kirk Session minute books and the very fabric of the building, Ross brings stories to amuse, delight and surprise! Here are tales of a missing cupboard, a black pulpit, and the generosity of Mary, Queen of Scots. We hear of the engineers who changed the Highlands in the eighteenth and nineteenth centuries, of the tragedy and chaos of the wars of the twentieth century, and of the close connections between Town and Kirk.

I've discovered that a predecessor preached to the town's defenders during a clan attack; that another needed government soldiers to allow him to take possession of his church; and that the preaching of another was described by the venerable Lord Cockburn as 'two and a quarter hours of sheer absolute nonsense'. All of which puts any contemporary ecclesiastical troubles into perspective!

Christianity is an historical faith. In an age which sometimes has little sense of history, Christians live by the stories of the Bible, and the best of their tradition, in order to live faithfully in the present and to have hope for the future. When showing people around the Old High, I sometimes say that it has been a Celtic, Roman Catholic and Episcopal Church, and that it is currently Presbyterian! All the major Christian communities of Inverness have their roots in this site, which properly belongs not simply to the congregation of Old High St Stephen's, but to all the citizens of the Highland Capital, for it helped to make us who we are.

Thank you Ross, for this wonderful volume which lets the stones tell their story!

Rev Peter W Nimmo BD ThM,
Minister of Old High St Stephen's Parish Church

For more information about Old High St Stephen's, please visit
www.oldhighststephens.com

INDEX

THE ESSAYS

INTRODUCTION

This collection of essays is not intended to be a history of the Old High Church. Indeed there already exists a summary guide to the Church and its history, originally researched and written by the Reverend F.J.L. Maclachlan, minister here from 1950 to 1963, and subsequently updated. The guide is strictly factual, and in my essays I have tried to provide some selective background information in a more entertaining form.

My basis of selection of topics for the essays has been very much personal choice, in particular dealing with aspects of our church's past and present which are not widely known, and which may be of interest to members and visitors to our lovely church.

The Old High Church is of great antiquity, and perhaps inevitably, particularly pre-reformation there are many tantalising gaps and inconsistencies in the information available. Perhaps my humble efforts may stimulate research into some of these areas.

Much of the Burgh Records are written in "Broad Invernessian Scots" with some mediaeval Latin thrown in for good measure. Where the meaning of the original is not readily clear to the modern reader, I have tried to provide, if not a translation, at least an indication of the meaning so far as I can make it out!

I have incorporated two essays which were originally intended for the use of Church members acting as guides to visitors.

My essays do not refer in any depth to our wonderful Father Willis Organ as Jim Monro has produced a separate masterly account of its history and recent restoration.

This booklet could not have been produced without the encouragement and support of the Minister and Kirk Session of Old High St Stephen's Church of Scotland, which I gratefully acknowledge. The front cover illustration is from an original painting by Gordon Harvey, who has also given valuable advice on the photographs.

Finally, I accept responsibility for errors, omissions, and wrong conclusions which no doubt will be found and pointed out!

Ross Martin, Inverness, 2013

Ross Martin is a senior Elder in Old High St. Stephen's Church, having been a member of the Old High since 1950. A law Graduate of Edinburgh University, he is also a Fellow of the Society of Antiquaries of Scotland.

1. OF CHAPELS AND ALTARS

Slezers 'Prospect of ye town of Inverness' published in 1693, and the sketches showing the Parish Church prior to 1700, including the map by James Gordon of Rothiemay held in the National Library of Scotland show various building extensions to the north and south of the main building of the Parish Church, and presumably these at least in part constitute separate Chapels within the Church, each served by a separate Chaplain.

It seems clear that the following Altars, some with their own chapels, were situated in the Parish Church of St. Mary :- The High Altar of the Blessed Virgin Mary; the Altar of the Holy Cross; the Altar of St Catherine the Virgin; the Altar of St. Michael the Archangel; and the Altar of St. John the Baptist. Parcels of land were granted for the support of various Altars, Chapels and their Chaplains.

Around 1190, however, King William the Lion granted to the Church of St. Thomas of Arbroath and to the Monks therein, the Church of Inverness with the Chaplaincy lands and tiends of every kind (in common with the assets of 32 other churches). The Abbey of Arbroath persistently starved the Kirk of funds thereafter, although it made grants to the preaching friars (Black Friars) of Inverness. The rental dues paid to Arbroath Abbey by the Church of Inverness were mainly in the form of herrings and salt.

This situation would have contributed to the establishment of chapels independent of the Parish Kirk, as these chapels would have had the ability to manage their own endowments and income outwith the influence of Arbroath Abbey. The subject of the location of altars and chapels is very confusing, with numerous conflicting and vague descriptions. Certainly the Chapel which stood within the present Chapel Yard, dedicated to the Blessed Virgin Mary of the Green was in existence in 1361, and indeed the Town Magistrates used it as a meeting place until 1563. It seems that both the Parish Church and the Chapel of the Green were used for Council business, as the election of Provost, baillies and councillors was held at the Chapel in 1559, and the corresponding election in 1561 took place in the Parish Church. There are references in old deeds to St. Thomas' Chapel, thought to have stood to the south east of Rose Street, the Chapel of Brigend in Bridge Street, and 'the Kirk called the Ravelstri', which seems to have been situated close by the Parish Kirk.

Cromwell's army, in Inverness from 1652, utilised stones from the ruined Chapel in the Chapel Yard and from the ruins of the Black Friars' Monastery in the building of the Citadel and Inverness Harbour.

2. OF RUBBLE AND MORTAR

The little hill on which the present Old High Church stands has been known as St Michael's Mound for many centuries. It is generally accepted that this is the spot on which Saint Columba preached to King Brude and his Pictish people in 565A.D. The first Christian church would of course have been a temporary structure, probably of wood, and so it is not surprising that no trace remains.

Eventually the Catholic Church built a more substantial building, and by 1171 the Church of Saint Mary in Innerness is referred to in a charter granted by King William the Lion. By 1371 the church roof required repairs, but at the time the building as a whole was described by the Bishop of Moray as 'a noble, strong and distinguished place.' It is not surprising that roof repairs were required from time to time as the church roof was thatched as least as late as 1558. The medieval Church was larger than the present Old High, and the church that had been constructed in perhaps the early 14th Century, contained a nave, north and south aisles, and a choir. Its dimensions were considerably altered in the seventeenth century.

Through the Middle Ages, the population of Inverness was expanding, and with it the congregation. In 1618 the Parish of Inverness was united with the Parish of

Bona (at that time the smallest parish in Scotland) and despite the establishment of a Second Charge, it was agreed that the congregation had outgrown the Church building and an addition was planned. By reconstructing the High Church, particularly the Choir and the transepts, a site was made available for the construction of a new church. This was to be known variously as the New, Irish, or Gaelic Church. At this time the terms Gaelic and Irish were interchangeable in describing the language we now know as Gaelic. The new church was built in 1649. *(It was rebuilt in 1792 - 93; reconstructed in 1822; became a Free Church, later altered in 1885 - 87; and now Leakey's Bookshop)*

Queen Anne had expressed concern in the years before 1706 for the Irish inhabitants of Inverness. The estimated population over the age of 14 years in Inverness at this time was 4000, and of these, some 3000 were only able to speak Gaelic:-'Therefore We of our Royal Bounty and for our interest for the Church and zeal for the promotion of the true religion----recommend a third minister be appointed to assist in the teaching of the Irish Gaelic members of the congregation.' The Queen supported the patronage of the third minister by a gift of land in Morayshire.

The collegiate structure of the Parish ministry gave rise to practical complications. After the establishment of the Second Charge in 1640, a third minister was appointed as an assistant in 1642 - 45 'because the Second Charge minister was ignorant of the Irish language.' This arrangement was short-lived, because he was translated to the First Charge in 1645 and the Third Charge was not formally created until 1704, after a gap of 59 years. Only the Irish language could be used in the New Church ; in the High Church only the English language could be used; the Minister and congregation could use both buildings, but were obliged to adhere to the language appropriate to the specific building.

But things had to change!

Between 1661 and 1689, when the Episcopalians were in the ascendant, it was reported " One part of the Church is used for the English Kirk and another for the Eirsche Kirk, and when a chaplain was here they had Church of England Service in one of them at another hour"

The High Church Inverness Scheme of 1929 quotes from a Deed of 1769 "the Old Kirk some years ago having been declared insufficient, the Presbytery of the Bounds threatened a prosecution against the Town Council and Heritors for building a new one, and the Kirk having been deserted, several inconveniences arise therefrom, such as that for the greatest part of the year the English and Irish Congregations meet but once a day and occupy the New or Irish Church by turns, and the rest of the year the Irish Congregation is exposed to the inclemency of the weather by attending public worship in the churchyard"

Eventually plans for a new Church were approved, and it was built between 1770 and 1772 at a cost of £1450. This is basically the Old High Church as it is today. The completed church could accommodate 1860 persons, but it is not recorded how many of these were seated in pews! Funding was provided by a loan from the Town Council, but Sir Hector Munro, M.P. for Inverness Burghs donated £1000 to reduce the debt. The church was re-roofed and extended at the end of the nineteenth century, and it was at this time that the Henry Willis Organ was installed.

A further church building as distinct from the Chapels, was in existence at the time of the Reformation. It was known as the Ravelstri, and various oblique references are made to it in the Burgh Records around that time. The Burgh Court books on 28 October 1570 refer to an action by the Burgh treasurer against George Cuthbert's widow for the warstay (cupboard) which sometime lay in the Ravelstri for keeping the ornaments (which Provost Cuthbert had allegedly diverted to his personal use.)

In the introduction to Records of Inverness, the author states 'there was also the Kirk called the Ravelstri which stood near the Parish Church, perhaps on or near the site of the present Gaelic Church : and he also refers to effect of the Reformation in the dilapidation of the Monastery, the Chapel of the Green, and the Ravelstri. A footnote explains that Ravelstri or ravestri means vestry of a church from the French *revestiaire*.

In 1568 the Burgh lets to Hendre Kar, younger, Burgess of Innernis, the house in the kirk yard behind the kirk, called the Ravelstri, at an annual rent of twenty six shillings and eight pennies, money of this realm.

This is the last reference to the Ravelstri.

3. LITTLE PEACE IN THE BURGH !

In the Middle Ages, Inverness was seldom peaceful as the following instances show.

In 1428, Alexander Macdonald of The Isles was summoned with another 40 chiefs to appear before King James I and his parliament in Inverness. When they appeared before the throne, they were seized and thrown into the dungeon pit. Most were quickly released. But Alexander remembered the treachery and when King and Parliament had gone, he came back and burned Inverness to the ground, one of seven bonfires that the Macdonalds allegedly lit on that ground in their clan's riotous history!

In 1689, Viscount Dundee, commander of King James VII's forces, had ridden to the Highlands. There the Macdonalds of Keppoch, indifferent to Orange or Stuart factions, but conducting a deadly feud against the Mackintoshes, were holding the Town of Inverness to ransom.

The Kirk Session Register records :-
28th Aprille 1689

"That day sermon preached be Mr Gilbert Marshall in the forenoone at the Cross, and that by reason Cole Macdonald was about the town boasting to com in with his whole force consisting of 8 or 900 men, to plunder the toun. Afternoone, Mr Mackenzie preached as aforesaid, all the citizens being necessitate to stand in a posture off Defence"

(Commenting on the above, the late Dick Milne observed- an early example of chaplains to the Forces)

(The Rev Mr Mackenzie was First Minister from 1688 to 1719, and the Rev Mr Marshall, Second Minister from 1674 to 1691)

Dundee bought the Macdonalds off with a ransom of 2700 pounds Scots, subscribed by the townspeople. Coll Macdonald, however, took umbrage at being called a common robber by Dundee, refused to join Dundee's Jacobite army, and led his force off down the Great Glen to their home country of

Lochaber! Dundee was meantime being pursued by King William's army commanded by General Mackay and having failed to obtain reinforcements, he rode south on May 8th leaving Inverness to be garrisoned by Mackay's army. The pursuit continued, however, and on 27th July Mackay's army was defeated, but Dundee was killed, at the Battle of Killiecrankie.

4. POST-REFORMATION RELIGIOUS COMINGS AND GOINGS, AND A SELECTIVE CHRONOLOGY OF TWO TURBULENT CENTURIES

1560 is considered to be the date of Reformation in Scotland, when the First Book of Discipline was drawn up, and Catholicism was replaced by Protestantism.

The existing vicar of the Parish Church in 1560 was George Hepburne, of whom little is known except that he may have been one of the illegitimate sons of the Bishop of Moray. He was replaced by the first Protestant Minister, one David Rag, previously a friar, and thus described as a pulpit-flitter. He had a roving eye, and a dubious reputation with the husbands of some married ladies. He lasted to 1565, when Thomas Howieson or Houston was appointed minister.

And what was the fate of the displaced Catholic clergy? They appear to have been reasonably well treated, as one-third of the income of the old church was used to pay the salaries of the Protestant clergy, and the remainder to support those of the former clergy who had renounced papacy and accepted the reformed religion.

In 1563 Robert Pont was sent north as a Commissioner of the General Assembly, and laboured here for five years. After this (largely because he could not speak Gaelic) he was ordered to another place "where his labours are expected to be more fruitful". Robert's son Zachary married John Knox's daughter and his son Timothy was the famed cartographer.

And Now For Some Dates!

1560	REFORMATION - Papal Authority abolished and mass made illegal by Scottish Parliament.
1561	First Book of Discipline approved *(Sets out detailed rules concerning the doctrine and administration of the Presbyterian Church in Scotland)*
1578	Second Book of Discipline *(Further detailed rules for the management and administration of the Kirk and its relations with Civil Authorities)*
1591	James VI grants Inverness the Great Charter of the Burgh
1592	Act of Parliament confirming liberties, privileges and immunities of the Kirk. Episcopal jurisdictions abolished and government of Kirk given to presbyteries, synods and General Assembly. (the Golden Act)
1610	Commencement of 30 years Episcopacy, with Bishops nominally controlling a religious environment not materially different from Presbyterianism.
1611	Publication of 'King James' Bible
1618	Parish of Bona united with Inverness
1638 - 40	Second Charge established
1638	National Covenant , which effectively condemned the Episcopal Church and reinforced the Church of Scotland's independence of the King, (Charles I)
1641	Episcopacy abolished by Act of Parliament which restored the Act of 1592
1643	Solemn League and Covenant, aimed to reform the Church of England to the Scottish Presbyterian pattern. King Charles II signed in 1650. Westminster Confession framed and ratified.
1649	Gaelic Church built : Patronage abolished

1651	Cromwell took possession of Inverness
1660	Cromwell dies : Episcopacy re-established, the King having reneged on signing the Covenant.
1661 - 1689	Episcopacy again in the ascendant, with Bishops reintroduced in 1662
1688 - 1702	Pages for this period cut out of Presbytery records!
1690	Presbyterianism re-established
1691	'A Presbyterian being appointed to the vacant Parish Church, the Magistrates who favoured episcopacy prevented his being placed for some time. Duncan Forbes, a zealous whig, attempting to force his way into the church along with the new minister, on the day fixed for placing him, was driven back from the doors, which were strongly guarded by armed men. The Government upon this sent a regiment to the town to support the Presbyterians.'
1702	Queen Anne to the throne
1703	Adult population of Inverness reckoned at 4000, of whom 3000 speak only gaelic
1704 - 06	Queen Anne sympathises with Irish worshippers and the Third Charge is established
1705	Presbyterian Library established in Inverness
1711	Patronage restored by Patronage Act
1724	Library, known as the Kirk Session Library, augmented by mortification from Dr James Fraser, the Royal Hospital, Chelsea covering gifts from his brother and himself.
1763	Reverend Murdach Mackenzie is presented to the First Charge by The Crown. This appears to be the first occasion on which the Crown exercised its powers of patronage

5. PERFECT ATTENDANCE

Attendance at Kirk was a subject to which the Town Council gave much thought.

In the Burgh Court Records, an Ordinance of 18th March 1564 can be roughly translated from the <u>very</u> broad Scots tongue in which it is written 'Every inhabitant of this burgh with their family and servants shall resort and convene to the Parish Kirk every Sunday to the exhortation and catechism at 10am and 3pm, and be found there before the last of the three ringings of the bell. And there with all humility and quietness make their prayers and hearken to the Word of God and not remove till the same be ended.' Anyone failing to comply shall pay a fine on a scale ranging from one shilling for the first offence to ten shillings for the fourth and subsequent offences.

In November 1574, however, Mr Thomas Howstoun, minister of the Burgh appeared before the magistrates asking that four Officers shall pass throughout the whole town on the Sabbath Day, charging every person to appear within the Parish Kirk from the third bell until preaching be done, under pain of a fine of 5 shillings payable to the Common Good, and to note the absentees, the said Officers themselves under pain of a fine of twenty shillings if they do not do their duty.

There is some evidence that lasting out in the kirk until the preaching of the Word of God was done, could on occasion be something of an ordeal!

Captain Edmund Burt in his Letters writes of a minister whose long supplications in a sing-song drawl were 'so remarkably flat and productive of horror that a master of music set them to his fiddle, and the wag used to say, that in the most jovial company, after he had played his tune but once over, there was no more mirth among them for the rest of that evening'

Lord Cockburn as a High Court Judge attended service in the Parish Church and records in his Journal of 1839 "Our sermon was by a worthy fanatic called Dr C…. There are few things more curious than the decorous appearance of patience with which sensible people can sit and hear a man, with an unattractive manner, roar out two and a quarter hours of sheer absolute nonsense ."

6. 1746 – THE AFTERMATH OF CULLODEN

The Church buildings and graveyard were much involved with the incarceration of prisoners around the time of the Battle of Culloden although the records are not entirely clear.

Apparently, prior to the battle, prisoners from the Government Army were held captive "in the church". We read "the Duke of Cumberland on taking possession of the town, appointed Captain Campbell of Lord Semple's Edinburgh Regiment, Town Major, and his Company of grenadiers became Town Guards. The Duke's next job was to liberate the Royalist prisoners who had been confined in the Town Church." The Duke gave them each a guinea, ordering his troops to take good care of them.

As to the Jacobite prisoners after the Battle, they were imprisoned in the 'Town Kirk', but precisely where is unclear. The Parish Church was in ruinous condition, and presumably not sufficiently secure to confine prisoners, and so the Gaelic Church was commandeered as a jail. Historian Seton Gordon quotes Captain Willie Mackay, a noted Invernessian Scholar as saying that the Jacobite prisoners were confined in the Tower of the Church. Probably both locations were used.

Among the Jacobite prisoners captured, were found some 36 deserters from the Royal Army, who had gone over to the Prince's side at various times. After a court-martial, these were shot in batches in the churchyard. Certainly other prisoners were executed in the churchyard. Two gravestones can be seen, near the west door of the Church, one with two curved hollows and the other with a V-shaped groove. They are in a direct line and nine paces apart. It is thought that the prisoner, blindfolded, sat or stood or knelt on the stone with two hollows whilst the musket of the executioner rested on the groove of the other. Possible marks of musket balls which missed the target can be seen on the wall in line with these stones.

There are more readily visible apparent marks of musket balls on the wall beside the tower door, and this would be consistent with the tradition that the wounded Government soldiers in Balnain House, which was used as a hospital, witnessed the executions.

Seton Gordon also observed 'against the wall of the Church other Jacobite prisoners were shot.'

The tradition is that the bodies of the prisoners shot in the graveyard were buried under the path leading to the west porch, by the tree.

7. A ROYAL PRESENTATION

Royal Presentation of Mr Alexander Fraser to be Minister of the
First Charge fifteenth January 1801.

Mr Patrick Grant had been admitted by the Presbytery to be Minister of the Town and Parish of Inverness on 2nd September 1800, after a series of disputes as to who had the right of Presentation of a minister to the vacancy. Two months later, however, Mr Grant submitted a Presentation from the Hon. Archibald Fraser of Lovat in his favour to be Minister of Kiltarlity and Convinth, and in due course was appointed to that Charge!

The First Charge of Inverness was thus again vacant within a few months, and the patronage this time fell to The Crown. A Royal Presentation in favour of Mr. Alexander Fraser, Second Minister of Inverness to be the Minister of the First Charge of the Town and Parish of Inverness was submitted to the Presbytery, who sustained it and forthwith translated him from the Second Charge to the First Charge on 5th March 1801. He remained Minister of the First Charge until his death in 1821.

This is the background to the manuscript Deed of Presentation, signed on behalf of King George the Third which is held in the Old High Church.

8. TOWN AND CHURCH

Over the centuries there was a strong relationship between the Town in the form of the Burgh Council and Magistrates on the one hand, and the Kirk, latterly in the form of the Minister and Kirk Session of the Parish Church, on the other.

Prior to The Reformation, the Council held meetings and elections in many locations, including the Chamber of the Tolbooth, The Provost's room, Chapel of the Black Friars, Chapel of the Blessed Virgin Mary of the Green, Chapel of the Bridgend, and the Parish Church.

Post Reformation, it was the custom of the Council to meet at the Provost's house every Sunday and process to the Kirk for the morning service. After the service they returned to the Provost's house for Hollands and bread and cheese, then returned, fortified, to Kirk for the afternoon service. This arrangement apparently continued to 1894, after which the attendance dropped to the annual Kirking ceremony.

There was frequent commonality between Council and Kirk Session. For instance, in 1674, the Kirk Elders consisted of the Provost, the four Bailies, two former Provosts, three former Bailies, the Dean of Guild, the Burgh Treasurer, and six Lairds!

In addition to its spiritual responsibilities, the Church looked after the moral and social welfare of the community.

Under the head of moral discipline, the areas of interest to the Church, carried out by the Elders, were diverse, including cases involving paternity, adultery, debauchery, fornication, cursing and swearing, and fishing on the Lord's Day. The enforcement of moral discipline was at its most intense in the years following the Reformation. The Session noted for instance that cursing and swearing reached a weekly peak on Fridays, market day, and elders were appointed to patrol the market in the hope of improving matters.

Arrangements for punishing misdemeanours were generally pragmatic, the Kirk Session dealing with offenders by means of disgracing them in various ways, such as standing in sackcloth at the Kirk door, or standing on the cockstool, which was first built in 1693. Failure to meet penalties imposed by the Session could involve being handed over to the magistrates for corporal punishment.

Particularly in the seventeenth and eighteenth centuries, accusations of witchcraft were common, and those accused were normally brought before the Presbytery for trial, rather than the magistrates. This spared them the extreme punishment and torture inflicted on those accused in other parts of Scotland, and indeed in some recorded cases in Inverness.

In 1662 Mr James Sutherland, minister, is summoned to a Town Council meeting to discuss taking "ane effectual course with the witches that ar presently in hand" Some weeks later he is recorded as joining Baillies and Councillors to "heir and try the witches presentlie in waaird, iff they will adheir to ther former confessionis, and to try of them quhat furder (what further) they will confesse"

Despite the rigorous enforcement of moral discipline, considerable compassion was shown by the Kirk Session to those in need, and there are numerous references to care being taken of foundling children. Collections were taken for deserving causes, both at home and overseas.

The situation of beggars was a constant cause of concern to both Council and Kirk Session.

In 1718 it was the Law of the Land that incomers from another part of the Kingdom should produce testimonials concerning their former good behaviour before settling in a new locality. Implementation of this law seems to have been ineffective in Inverness, for in 1720, the Burgh Records report that the town was oppressed by 'strange beggars who come in great multitudes from other parishes and provinces to the great prejudice of the poor of the place' The Kirk Session and the Council combined to provide badges to those identified as the native poor of the place, and 35 badges were distributed in 1722.

In 1792 the Kirk Session recommended to the ministers to request the congregation to regard these poor persons to whom badges are given as objects of their charity.

Beggars apart, the welfare of the poor of the Burgh was a source of constant concern to both Council and Session. Despite the terms of provost Dunbars settlement of the Hospital to the Kirk Session in 1683, the magistrates let the property in various ways over the next 150 years, and it was only from about 1845 to the building of the Poor-house at Muirfield in 1861 that part of Dunbar's hospital was used for the benefit of the poor.

9. WHAT'S IN A NAME ?

The first written reference to a church on the site of the present Old High is in a charter granted by William the Lion between 1164 and 1171, reading 'William, by the grace of God King of Scots to all good men in his whole land, Greetings: Know that I have given and granted to God and the Church of Saint Mary in Inuirnys, and Thomas, Priest, parson of the said church, one plough of land in perpetual mortification -----'

Around 1190, however, William granted the church and its revenues to the monastery of Arbroath, whose Abbots thereafter consistently starved it of funds. Nevertheless by 1371 the Church was described by the Bishop of the Diocese as 'a noble, strong and distinguished place', though its roof was in disrepair.

After the Reformation in 1560, the name of St Mary is quietly dropped, the church being referred to as the Parish Church or the High Church. With the increase in population of the town, the congregation was outgrowing the building, and in 1641 major rebuilding resulted in the existing church building being split in two, with the Irish or Gaelic Church being built roughly on the site of what is now Leakey's bookshop. As services were conducted in gaelic in the Gaelic Church, and those in the Parish Church were conducted in English, the Old High was for a time known as the English Church.. The name of St Mary's revived in the full name of St Mary's Gaelic Church, now Dalneigh and Bona Church of Scotland.

By the beginning of last century, our church was officially and simply known as the High Church of Inverness. The introduction of 'Old' into its title arose from the Union in 1929 of the Church of Scotland and the United Free Church. This was necessary because both the Church of Scotland and the UF church had a High Church in Inverness. We became the Old High and by a strange historical twist, the UF High Church became St Columba High Church.

The official intimation to our congregation read "The change, as it affects us, is slight in form, and in substance it only emphasises the antiquity of our title. Any regret is only outweighed by the satisfaction that the problem has been met and overcome in a spirit of Christian goodwill and harmony."

The Old High Church in Winter

Communion Silver

Gravestone Slab

Kings Colour of the 6th Battalion,
Queens Own Cameron Highlanders

Stained Glass Window

The Martinpuich Cross

The Curfew Bell

Newel Staircase in the Tower

The Two Doors in the Tower

The Kirk Spire in 1978

The Robertson Mausoleum

Frieze Decorated with Symbols of Mortality

Entrance to the Mausoleum

Floor Slab with more Grizly Symbols of Mortality

The Paupers Coffin in the Tower

The Graveyard seen from the Tower

The Gravestones used in Executions after Culloden

The Groove which held the Musket

The Grooves which held the Prisoners Elbows

Kirk and City -
Minister and Council Officer

From 1971, the Old High Church and its daughter Church, St Stephen's were established as a linked charge. In October 2003, the two churches were united as Old High St. Stephen's Church of Scotland, with both buildings retained for worship.

10. THE REFORMATION
A 16TH CENTURY LAND GRAB

In 1560, the Roman Catholic religion was abolished as that of the State.

With the Reformation under way, Mary, Queen of Scots, whatever her own religious inclinations were, took good care at first to tread in the paths of the new Protestant majority as most of her peers had accepted the new faith.

In 1562 Queen Mary visited Inverness. and again in 1567, when she made a grant of all the churches, chapels and church lands with all lands and fishings which formerly pertained to the Dominican or preaching Friars of our said Burgh, to the Provost, Baillies Council and Community of Inverness to maintain Ministers and readers and other ecclesiastical burdens, repair broken down places and convert them into hospitals for the poor and needy.

The Burgh authorities, however, lost no time in selling and feuing parts of the lands thus acquired to their own number at very advantageous rates. In 1574 they formally granted a charter of lands, lately belonging to the Friars, to Provost William Cuthbert, first as a lease, subsequently converted to a feu. In the same year Cuthbert got the feu of the former school, and induced the Council to repair the riverside to prevent flooding of his new property. 1575 they let a bundle of properties to Robert Vaus, burgess of Inverness, and his male heirs. The Cuthbert family held on to the Priory lands until 1640, when they were reclaimed by the Presbytery to form a new manse and glebe.

11. THE REFORMATION
PROVOST GEORGE CUTHBERT AND
THE FRIARS' MISSING CUPBOARD

The Reformation in Scotland followed a rather more peaceful course than was found elsewhere in Europe, but nevertheless, as it gained momentum, pressure on the Catholic Church increased.

On 23rd June 1559, the Prior and Black Friars of Inverness felt obliged to deposit their charters and ornaments, including several silver-gilt chalices, with the Provost and Magistrates of Inverness. Provost George Cuthbert and two baillies signed a receipt which included an undertaking to hand them back when better times returned. When John McGilleywe, one of the baillies, signed his name, it was followed by the words 'at the pen led by George Cuthbert'. Provost George died soon after this event.

Fast forward to December 1561, and the magistrates are demanding from provost George's son the return of the friars assets which were in George's possession at the time of his decease. Various items are specified, mostly kept in a great 'waestaye' or cupboard, and the 'keis of the Stepill' are also sought.

By 7 February 1562 the baillies who witnessed the receipt for the friars assets are in court pressing Provost George's widow to admit that she had in her possession after George's death, the Chalice and ornaments from the friars. They were apparently unsuccessful.

Eventually in October 1570, the Burgh Court Books record an action against George Cuthbert's widow by the Burgh Treasurer on the grounds that Provost George had wrongly and illegally removed to his own house the warstay in which the ornaments which pertained to the town of Inverness were kept, and ordering the widow to deliver the warstay to the council house on the following Tuesday without fail. As in the case of the other actions, no outcome is recorded, and the assumption is that even if it was delivered on that Tuesday, when the Treasurer got there, the warstay was bare!

Most commentators conclude that the Cuthbert family denied throughout, all knowledge of the whereabouts of both the Friars warstay and its valuable contents, which have not been heard of since!

12. THE ROBERTSON OF INSHES MAUSOLEUM

This is situated just north of the entrance steps in what had been the south transept of the mediaeval church. The rectangular enclosure has columned screen walls with a frieze decorated with symbols of mortality.

The Robertson family were major landowners in Inverness for about 400 years until the 1880's. In 1663 William Robertson, one of the movers and shakers of seventeenth century Inverness petitioned the Kirk Session for permission to build a tomb for his grandmother's body. The Kirk Session feared that his plan might mean loss of light in the Kirk, and after discussion with the Bishop of Moray, it was agreed that if the Kirk Session's fears proved well founded, the memorial could be reduced to a more acceptable height. The mausoleum was built by James Gordon and William Durham in 1664-65.

Over the doorway is a latin inscription indicating that here was buried in 1660, Mary Purves, mother of Janet Sinclair, .wife of John Robertson of Inshes. (presumably the aforesaid grandmother). To the left is a blank shield with initials MWR (Master William Robertson) and date 1665, and to the right is the Sinclair coat of arms and initials IS (Janet Sinclair). On the side wall of the mausoleum is a memorial tablet under an ornate pediment and flanked by badly damaged columns with the initials HR, MH, and SF and a latin inscription referring to Hugh Robertson, buried here in 1707. He had been three times Provost of Inverness.

On the ground is the graveslab of William Robertson, d.1682, carved with a coat of Arms and more grizly reminders of death! William Robertson in 1676 had obtained permission from the Session to erect two pews next to the Guildry desk for the use of his family. In return for this he gifted to the Kirk "the little desk belonging sometime to his mother" "Little" was something of an understatement, as it originated as an auctioneers desk in Holland, and became the ornate pulpit in the Gaelic Church, where it was described as an "old and elegantly carved oak pulpit", known as "the Black Pulpit".It was eventually removed when the Gaelic Church became the Free Church, and sadly was destroyed in 1966 by vandals when in store.

13. THE FLANDERS GRAVESTONE

This grave slab which lies between the projections for the West Porch and the Choir Apse is distinguishable by its considerable size, light colour, and the lead sockets which held a brass plate. The initials AR CS inscribed on the stone are presumably of later date.

The stone was originally a polished slab of Tournais stone into which was set a monumental brass of a specific design which would have included two figures with their heads resting on pillows, and further engraved surrounds with the lines filled with red and black mastic. Such rare examples of brass matrix stones in Scotland were imported from Flanders in the late fourteenth or early fifteenth century.

The lead sockets which held the brass plates are still clearly preserved. Could a clue to the provenance of the stone be the reference in the Records of Inverness to the removal by 'the scollaris of the scule' of brass on 'the stane of the hie alter and new ile within the kirk of Innernis' at the time of the Reformation.

--- 'the scholars of the school' --- 'the stone of the high altar and new aisle within the kirk of Inverness'

It also seems possible that the stone, presently lying outside the Church is in its original position within the mediaeval Church, but exposed to the open air when the church was subject to rebuilding in a changed format involving resiting of the walls in the seventeenth century.

14. OLD HIGH CHURCH WAR MEMORIAL

The memorial to the fallen in the two World Wars is on the wall outside the Organ Apse. The names of those killed in the 1914 - 18 war total 61, and in the 1939 - 45 war 9. In the first World War, some 406 men and 26 women from the congregation served : 85 were wounded, 4 were prisoners of war, and 25 medals and mentions in dispatches were awarded.

The memorial was designed by Mr Samuel G Alexander and executed by Mr W.R. Cumming of D&A Davidson, (grandfather of Miss Janice Cumming)

Dedication of the memorial took place on Armistice Day 1921, the honour of unveiling was assigned to Mrs Roderick MacLean, Clifton Lodge, and Mrs William Robertson, Isle View, both of whom lost three sons in the war.

Miss Janice Cumming and the writer have a further connection with the Memorial in that both our fathers were partners in the firm of Roderick MacLean & Company, Chartered Accountants. Roderick MacLean, who founded the firm was the eldest of Mrs MacLean's five sons who all saw active service in the first World War. He ended the War as Second in Command of the Sixth Camerons. His only surviving brother, Evan, serving in the Royal Flying Corps, was shot down and badly wounded. The writer can remember meeting him on his farm in Easter Ross in the 1950's.

15. TO THE TOWER

The West Tower is the oldest part of the Church building and the lowest section arguably constitutes the oldest surviving construction in the city.

There is much speculation amongst historians as to the age of the tower, the lower section being variously attributed to the 14th, 15th, and 16th centuries. The higher section culminating in the steeple is generally accepted as dating from the 17th century.

The lower, mediaeval part of the tower is substantial, square in plan, and battered (tapered) up to the level - clearly visible - when it was heightened in the 17th century. There is a slightly projecting mural newel staircase in the south-east corner, connecting the five stone vaulted floors, though at present only usable as an access between two of these. The top of the tower has a balustered parapet carried on corbels mixing with rainwater spouts, which may date from the repairs made in 1649, and is topped by a copper-sheathed spire. The stone corbel stones for the original timbers still exist inside the belfry under the parapet wall.

The tower is placed asymmetrically in relation to the west gable of the present church as a result of the widening of the church to the south in 1772.

The tower itself was essentially a bell tower and never could have been a central tower nor even an entrance porch. This is clearly shown by the limited dimensions of the tower and the smallness of the doorway.

There are two doors in the west aspect of the tower, one at ground level and a smaller one at first floor level. The purpose of the upper door is a matter of some conjecture. Access would have been by means of wooden steps or a retractable ladder – a common defensive arrangement, and this theory is supported by evidence of a drawbar to strengthen the door. The lower door must have been very substantial, to resist attack, and indeed to secure the vaulted ground floor chamber when it was in use as a prison, having no access to upper floors.

Although there is now no access from the tower to the Church itself, there could have been an access doorway at first floor level in mediaeval times, which has subsequently been filled in, possibly when the church was reconstructed prior to the building of the Gaelic Church in 1649. It has been suggested that in this event, the upper door could have led to a priest's room (there is an aumbry to hold sacred vessels inside the first floor doorway), or to a singers' gallery within the nave of the old church .

References to the High Church's name made it clear that this referred to the height of the tower rather than its services. After the Disruption in 1843 the Free Church and the United Presbyterian denominations built their own churches, and by the 1860's their chapels were nationally being rebuilt on a much larger and architecturally more ambitious scale, apparently in deliberate competition with the parish churches, often flaunting steeples in face of the Parish Church. The Old High is no longer highest in dimension!

The clock in the tower is the property of the City of Inverness, and shall 'be regarded and used as a public clock'

There are two bells in the tower, and in the 1929 High Church, Inverness Scheme, which regulates the transfer of the Old High Church building from the Burgh of Inverness to the Church of Scotland General Trustees, it is noted that the Burgh shall have right of access to the steeple of the said church and to the bells therein on all necessary occasions (except during the hours of Divine Service) and shall also have the right to have the said bells rung at the expense of the Burgh on weekdays at the hours at which they are at present in use to be rung -------.

On 7 October 1703 it is enacted that< the Church Bell be told every night at ten o'clock>, and on 26th December that year the treasurer was ordered to give the Kirk Officers <ane pound candles monthly during the long nights for toleing the church bell at 10 ocloack at night>

Further regulations regarding bell-ringing are included in the Kirk Session Records for 1720. The bells are to be rung at five am. in summer and six am. in winter ; and in the evening at both eight pm. and ten pm. throughout the year. The officers should have Thirty pounds Scots yearly (£2.50 sterling) for ringing the said bells at the said times. From that time the Church bell was rung manually every night from 1720 for curfew at 8pm apart from the years of World War II, (when the ringing of bells was to warn of an invasion!), up to 1999, when the office of bell ringer was replaced by an automatic system.

I have not been able to trace any reference to the reduction in the daily bell-ringing hours, but it appears that early morning bell-ringing continued for more than a century.

Judging by the remarks attributed to the bell ringer of the mid-19th century in 'Reminiscences of Inverness' by John Fraser, automation would have been doubly welcome then. Thomas Grant, the beadle is asked 'are you the bell ringer ?' and replies 'I am, and a driech job it is. Just fancy coming in here at the dead of winter for the purpose of awakening the drowsy breadwinners'

Grant was followed as bellringer by the Paterson 'dynasty', this family carrying out the duty for the ensuing century! Andrew Paterson, born 1841 had rung for 50 years when, on the occasion of his Golden Wedding, he handed on the duty to his son, Tom. For a period before the Second World War, Tom's nephew was bellringer, but had to give up following an injury at work, and after the war Tom resumed control of the bell-rope. Retiring in 1964, he was succeeded by Simon MacDonald, the final holder of the office.

The earlier of the two bells in the steeple dates from 1658, and was allegedly acquired from Fortrose Cathedral. It is inscribed <Johannes Burgeses Luys me fecit 1658. Soli Deo Gloria> The East Bell was cast by John Watt & Son, Glasgow, and is dated 1838.

Also in the Tower are the rather dilapidated remains of a wooden 'paupers' coffin with a removable lid. This was used particularly at times of epidemics to provide a burial where funds to provide an individual coffin were not available. The last recorded use of the coffin was at the time of the cholera epidemic in Inverness in 1849, when 112 townspeople died.

16. GRAVESTONE SLABS AND BURIALS INSIDE THE CHURCH

There are some sinister looking indentations in the carpeting in the west aisle of the Church, and the writer was able to examine those before the present carpeting was laid. There are two well-preserved slabs in the aisle leading from the pulpit to the west door:-

The inscription on the first reads as follows:-

HEIR LYS ROBERT HEBRONE SUMTIM BURGIS OF INVERNESS WHO DEPARTIT THE 2ND DAY OF AUGUST 1638 AND HIS SPOUSE MASDETTE COBRON.

The second inscription reads:-

HEIR LYS ANE HONEST MAN VILLIAM PATERSONE ELDER MERCHAND BURGESS OF INVERNESS AND MAGRAT PATERSONE HIS SPOUS.

The Paterson stone bears no date, but William Paterson Elder, burgess and Baillie features frequently in the Records of Inverness in the early years of the 17th century. The latest mention of his name is as attending a burgh court meeting on 25th October 1621.

Interestingly, on 14 October 1615, the Burgh Court Books refer to a decree to Johne Grant of Glenmoristoun and William Patersoun Elder merchand Burges of Inverness to flit and remove themselves and their families, tenants etc. from the burra hauch, which the Council considered they were illegally occupying. (Indeed, for an honest man, William made quite a few court appearances!)

It is surprising that these two burials <burial indicated by Heir Lys> took place within the church in the Seventeenth Century, considering that The First Book of Discipline, adopted by the Reformed church in 1560 ruled that burials within a church were unseemly, and should be carried out " in the most free air in a walled and fenced place kept for that use only."

Under the first radiator in the aisle leading from the east door, concealed by the carpet is a fascinating fragment of a burial stone. All that can be read of the inscription is HEIR LYIS ANE H--------- and OBIL AND MIGHTIE GEORG. There is also a coat of Arms clearly visible.

The details and photograph were referred to the Lyon King of Arms for identification, but Lyon was unable to identify it. Nor could he explain several puzzling features. The style 'Most Noble and Mighty' is that of an Earl. But the Arms of all the Scottish Earls are known and recorded, but these Arms are none of these. Lyon goes on to make various observations; the shape of the shield being highly eccentric and looks as if based on a late 15th century MS illustration of continental origin ; the Arms bear most resemblance to those of the Leslie Earls of Rothes, but the devices on the stone are not consistent with the Leslie Arms; and the only possible Earl George died in Dieppe in 1558, and can hardly be buried <HERE LYES> In Inverness! An Unsolved Mystery!

(The Records of Inverness Burgh Court contain a reference to an appeal on 22 May 1579 by Merchants of Hamburg against the arrestment of their ship and goods at the instance of the Nobill and Mychtie lord George Erle of Huntly, Lord Gordoun and Baidyenocht------ Any Connection?)

The Proceedings of the Society of Antiquaries of Scotland for 1998 record that when the floor of the Greyfriars Free Church Hall was being relaid in the 1990's, human remains probably from the medieval cemetery were found. Similar burials are likely to lie under the present Old High Church and Greyfriars Free Church (now Leakey's bookshop).
It is possible that structural remains of the medieval parish church still exist under the present church or in the cemetery.

17. VISITOR TOUR NOTES – OLD HIGH CHURCH INTERIOR

Enter by the East Door and turn into the first aisle - south wall on left.

First window dates from 1914 and depicts Our Lord carrying His Cross ; the Marys at the tomb.

Memorial brasses commemorate various members of the Wimberley family, distinguished soldiers associated with the Queens Own Cameron Highlanders.

The next stained glass window dates from 1893: Our Lord with doctors in the Temple ; St Paul on Mars Hill, and is in memory of the Rev Donald MacDonald.

Note brass in memory of Charles Fraser Mackintosh, M.P., a noted scholar and historian, author of 'Invernessiana'

Brass in memory of Captain JSR Macdonald, a grandson of the Rev Donald Macdonald.

The Apse and the chancel arch date from 1891, when the two porches were added.

The Organ, a two-manual instrument was built by Henry Willis, and has recently (2011) been comprehensively rebuilt.

The Communion Table and Choir Stalls are memorials to the Very Reverend Dr. Norman Macleod. Carvings on stall ends record that these stalls were presented by FW Grant of Maryhill, Inverness, in June 1914. Mr Grant was one of the Trustees of St. Stephens Church at the time it became independent of the Old High.

The Lectern was presented to the Church by a Mrs Douglas in 1918 in memory of her late husband, who had been agent of the County Bank. The Saints carved on the Lectern are St Andrew, St Peter, St Paul and St Columba, who in allusion to his founding the local Christian Mission, carries the small model of a church, with a dove perched on his shoulder.

The ironwork supporting the steps to the lectern is the work of the late Donnie Mann, blacksmith, whose family have been staunch members of the church for generations. In the east glass display case you can see the certificate of the first Communion taken by Daniel Mann, Donnie's grandfather. Daniel Mann, JP, was appointed Precentor and Choirmaster in 1891. *(the precentor's duty was to lead the congregation's singing by singing each line, normally of the psalm, for it to repeat. This practice dates back to times when literacy was by no means universal).* Daniel Mann was in office when the organ was installed, and as the position then became redundant, he was the last precentor in the Old High.

The floor of the Sanctuary is of Iona Marble, another symbolic link with St. Columba. The stained glass windows in the Chancel are, on the east, St. Michael, and on the west, Our Lord blessing little children. Both date from 1925.

To the west of the central area is a glass case displaying a first edition of the 1611 King James Bible, the 'He' version. This is the property of the Inverness Kirk Session Library. *(See separate essay)*

There are also two brass trays, one engraved 'Parish Church Inverness 1737'

Presently in the Church strong room is a 'very strong and curious iron chest' which was gifted to the Kirk Session in 1712, by the then Kirk Treasurer, James Thomson.

Continuing along the west aisle past the pulpit, the next window, a memorial to Lord Gordon, dating from 1899, is of Moses and Samuel.

Underneath is the Field Communion Set used by the Rev Donald Caskie, minister of the Scots Kirk in Paris who was known as 'The Tartan Pimpernel' as a result of his bravery in assisting allied prisoners to escape from occupied France in World War 2.

In the north-west corner of the interior hangs the Francis Perigal parliamentary clock, dated 1770, and so presumably has been in use since the rebuilt Church was opened in 1772.

The stained glass window in the centre of the north wall is a memorial to the Rev. Donald Macleod, depicting the Risen Christ with the Disciples on the Road to Emmaus. It dates from 1958, and is typical in its strong colours of the work of Gordon Webster.

There are three interesting memorial tablets nearby:- John Inglis died 1781 in America 'who was murdered by a band of ruffians while on a visit to a friend's house'

William Inglis, Provost of Inverness who died tragically in 1801,was the driving force behind the establishment of Inverness Royal Academy and The Royal Northern Infirmary.

Then the Duff of Muirtown memorial with its touching motto 'Kind heart be true and you shall never rue' A Duff died at Negapatam, and the strange monument on top of Fyrish Hill in Ross-shire represents the gates of this Indian City.

The last window in this aisle is the Cochrane Memorial, dating from 1916, depicting Our Lord at the well, and the Adoration of the Magi.

Outside the choir room on the west stair is a large and verbose monument to the Kennedy family. Note here the reference to James Grant Kennedy, who died carrying the Colours at Waterloo, only three days after his fifteenth birthday!

In the gallery are a few pews marked 'free seat' This dates back only forty years or so when seat rents were abolished. Prior to this seats in most pews were the preserve of those who paid a few shillings annually for the privilege of exclusive right of occupancy. In fact for many years if not centuries a dispute between the Town and the Church rumbled on as to the allocation of the rents as a result of the financing of the rebuilding of the Church in 1772. Up to 1811 the revenue from seat rents was £84 sterling per annum, and increased thereafter to £130 per annum. Apparently the seat rents were collected by the Burgh Council, and by 1882 at least £1300 had been accumulated by the

Council as surplus revenue from the High Church. The dispute was settled in 1929.

The free seats were for those too poor or unwilling to pay. It is interesting to see that these pews are the most heavily carved with initials- perhaps because it was not possible to identify which bored children sat there!

The seating at front centre of the gallery is in the form of armchairs. Until recent times when the Provost and Magistrates attended church, for the annual Kirking Ceremony or on National Occasions, they sat here in the 'breist o' the laft'. In front of each chair is a Bible, embossed in gold with the Burgh Arms, dated 1775.

The large window in the east wall (the Nativity of Our Lord) is signed by E P Howden, c.1890.

This concludes the interior tour, but visitors may be interested to look round the wall tablets, many referring to those who died abroad both on military and colonial service.

18. INSIDE THE OLD HIGH
AMPLIFICATION OF SOME REFERENCES IN THE TOUR
NOTES TO MEMORIALS IN THE CHURCH

There are memorial brasses for members of the Wimberley family, distinguished soldiers associated with the Queens Own Cameron Highlanders. Two members of the family deserve special attention. Firstly Captain Douglas Wimberley, born 1828 who took early retirement from the army after active service, and spent the last thirty-three years of his life in Inverness, carrying out much valuable research on the history of this Church, of which he was an elder. And secondly, his grandson Major-General Douglas Neil Wimberley, who commanded the 51st Highland Division in World War 2, from the battle of Alamein until the end of the campaign in Sicily. He became Colonel of the Regiment in 1951.

Brass plates refer to the Revd Donald MacDonald, D.D., He became Minister of the first charge in 1852 and died in 1892. The next brass plate is in memory of Capt. JSR MacDonald, Australian Field Artillery, killed in action in Flanders in 1917, aged 22. A second generation Australian, he had seen service in Gallipoli and the Middle East before his posting to France, he was a grandson of the aforementioned Revd Donald MacDonald.

The next brass plate is in memory of Charles Fraser-Mackintosh, a famous Highland scholar who combined research and authorship particularly regarding Inverness and the Highlands, with the duties of Member of Parliament, first for Inverness Burghs, (1874 to 1885) and subsequently for Inverness County (1885 to1892)

The stained glass windows in the apse are in memory of Duncan Shaw and his young son. Duncan Shaw was a member of the legal firm of Anderson Shaw and Gilbert, which is still in practice in Inverness

Two brass plates are in memory of Edward Strathearn, Baron Gordon of Drumearn. As the climax of an illustrious legal career, having been Solicitor General for Scotland and Lord Advocate he was made a Law Life Peer in 1876, and thereafter sat as a Lord of Appeal.

A marble plaque commemorates Major Ian Mackay. He was the brother of the late Captain Willie Mackay, a well known Inverness character, and a partner in the still existing firm of Innes and MacKay. Their family home was Craigmonie, now the Craigmonie Hotel.

On the east wall is a plaque in memory of the wife of Joseph Mitchell, Civil Engineer. Born in Forres in 1803, Joseph Mitchell received part of his education at Inverness Academy. He assisted Thomas Telford on the Caledonian Canal construction, became Inspector of the Highland Roads and Bridges 1824 - 1864, and engineer for the Highland Railway, in particular from Inverness to Perth Junction. He retired to London where he died in 1883.

Outside, in the east corridor, is a plaque commemorating the life of John Mitchell, father of the above Joseph, who rose from being a stonemason working for Thomas Telford to an engineering career as impressive as that of his son, who succeeded him as Principal Inspector when he died in 1824.

19. THE MARTINPUICH CROSS

The Martinpuich Cross is the centrepiece of the Queens Own Highlanders Memorial Area, created in 2013 to bring together various items relating to the close connection between the Regiment and the Old High, its Regimental Church.

The Battle of Martinpuich was an engagement in the Battle of the Somme in 1916. The Battle of the Somme is known as the greatest catastrophe of the First World War. On the first day of the Battle, British losses were over 57,000, of whom over 20,000 were killed.

On 14th September 1916, the 6th Battalion of the Queen's Own Cameron Highlanders' objective was the village of Martinpuich. The troops were unusually heavily laden, and had to cross extremely rough ground . The village was captured and about 190 prisoners taken. For the first time ever, tanks assisted the infantry in their advance. Care was taken to hide the tanks' approach from the enemy, and low-flying aircraft were used to drown the noise of the tanks' engines. The tanks were in action, but tank warfare was in its infancy :- of 49 tanks initially lined up, only 32 reached the start point, and of these, 9 failed to catch up with the infantry, a further 9 broke down, 5 were ditched in craters, leaving only 9 which actually accompanied the Camerons!

Before leaving the battle lines, a large wooden Celtic Cross was erected at the entrance to Martinpuich. The names of the fallen on standard metal labels were nailed below the inscription. The Cross bears 37 metal labels, and according to the Regimental Records, one man whose name was attached by mistake had the pleasure later of detaching his own.

A Cemetery grew around the spot, and although Martinpuich was recaptured by the Germans, the Cross was still standing after the Armistice, and brought to Inverness.

20. THE OLD HIGH COMMUNION CUPS

In 1802, John Baillie, an Inverness house carpenter bequeathed a legacy of Fifty Pounds to the Kirk Session of Inverness for the express purpose of being applied by them for the purchase of six silver Communion Element Cups.

These were made by Alexander Stewart, silversmith of Inverness, and are illustrated on p.157 of "Highland Gold and Silversmiths"

(There was a John Baillie, son of William Baillie of Dunain, Provost of Inverness 1691, born October 1713, who could have been the above carpenter, though he would have been 89 years of age at the time of his death. The Baillie family attended the High Kirk, and the Provost aforesaid's first wife was Mary, daughter of William Duff of Muirtown, another High Kirk family)

The silver cups replaced the six pewter Communion Cups (and plates) made by James Dallas of Inverness, which are now on loan to Inverness Museum.

Inverness Kirk Session Records state in 1763 "James Dallas, pewterer, being appointed to make 4 tin cups for the use of Sacrament occasions, he produced his accot. therefor, amounting to one pound ten shillings."

And again in 1778, the Session authorise the purchase of "eight pewter plates for the conveniency of holding the elements of bread for the Sacrament " and the payment of James Dallas, Pewtherer, for the same.

21. THE 'KING JAMES' BIBLE AND THE 'KIRK SESSION' LIBRARY.

The 1611 King James Bible is always described as forming part of the Kirk Session of Inverness Library, which includes it amongst its 3385 volumes, some dating from as early as 1529. The Bible, which is in the showcase in front of the pulpit, is a first edition, and is in **Black Letter**, with chapter headings in roman type. This edition is known as the 'Great 'HE' Bible' on account of the reading in Ruth 3, 15, where the translation is, 'and he went into the city.' The other issue or issues of the year 1611 translate 'and she went into the city.'

The Presbyterian Library of Inverness was established by order of the General Assembly of 1705.

The original collection, 'sent by piously disposed persons in the city of London', consisted of 200 books together with 30 copies of the Bible in Irish (at this time the Bible had not been translated into Scots gaelic). There were 105 donors in the first 10 years of the library's existence, including provosts and ex-provosts of Inverness, various citizens and merchants of the town, including skinners, peri-wig makers and, rather sinisterly, a commissar.

Then in 1724, James Fraser, for 40 years Secretary of the Royal Hospital in Chelsea, set up a Trust establishing the terms under which the donations of 1000 Scots merks (roughly £55) by himself in 1712, and 900 merks in 1718 by him as executor of his late brother, William, late Governor of Fort St George in the East Indies, for the benefit of the Library were to be carried out. The Frasers were sons of the Rev Alex Fraser of Petty, 1633 - 81.

In April 1719 the Kirk Session appointed Baillie Dunbar to remit the 'rents' which had accrued on his gift of 1000 merks, to Mr James Fraser in London in order for him to buy books, as specified on behalf of the Session. In August 1720, the session committee appointed to receive the books bought by Mr Fraser, reported that they had viewed all the books.

The 1611 King James Bible is marked 'Inverness 1719' on the flyleaf, and it would therefore appear to have been part of the 1719 consignment!

The terms of the Fraser Trust include both ministers and Magistrates in the conduct of the funds, and there have been various legal disputes as to their respective rights and duties over the years.

The location of the library, and the care and interest taken in its contents, has varied over the centuries, but it is now safely in the hands of Inverness City Library, with the exception of the King James Bible which we are proud to have on display here in the Old High Church.

22. COLOURS OF THE QUEEN'S OWN CAMERON HIGHLANDERS

The Colours now hanging from the Gallery in the centre of the Church are:-

1. The Colours of the 1st Battalion, presented by HM The Queen at Balmoral in 1955, transferred from Glasgow Cathedral and laid up and rededicated here on 4th May 2014.

2. The Colours of the 3rd Militia Battalion presented by The Mackintosh of Mackintosh at Fort George in 1909 and laid up on 19th September 1965.

3. The King's Colour of the 3rd (Special Reserve) Battalion, laid up on 19th September 1965.

4. The Colours of the 4th/5th Battalion, presented by HM King Edward VII in 1909 and laid up on 27 September 2015.

5. The King's Colour of the 6th (Service) Battalion presented by Lieut.General Sir Richard Butler at Braine-le-Comte on 21st January 1919, and laid up on 19th September 1920.

6. The King's Colour of the 7th (Service) Battalion presented by HRH the Duke of York at Cameron Barracks, Inverness on 17th September 1920 and laidup on 19th September 1920.

APPENDIX 1.
MINISTERS OF THE FIRST CHARGE, INVERNESS, FROM 1560

?1561	DAVID RAG
1567	REV. THOMAS HOUSTON OR HOWIESON
15??	REV. ALEXANDER CLARK (D.1635)
1605	REV. JAS. BISHOP, A.M.
1620	REV. WM. CLOGGIE, A.M.
1640	REV. MURDO MACKENZIE, A.M.
1645	REV. DUNCAN MACCULLOCH
1660	REV. JAMES SUTHERLAND, A.M.
1674	REV. ALEXANDER CLERK, A.M.
1683	REV. ANGUS MACBEAN, A.M.
1688	REV. HECTOR MCKENZIE
1720	REV. WILLIAM STUART
1727	REV. ALEXANDER MCBEAN, A.M.
1763	REV. MURDACH MACKENZIE, A.M.
1774	REV. ROBERT ROSE
1800	REV. PATRICK GRANT, A.M.
1801	REV. ALEXANDER FRASER, A.M.
1821	REV. THOMAS FRASER, A.M.
1834	REV. ALEXANDER CLARK
1852	REV. DONALD MACDONALD, D.D.
1890	VERY REV. DR. NORMAN MACLEOD
1907	REV. DONALD MACLEOD, M.C., T.D., B.D.
	The Rev. Donald Macleod retired as Minister of the First Charge in 1939 but remained as senior minister until 1955.
1939	REV. RODERICK MURCHISON M.A.
1950	REV. FRANCIS MACLAUCHLAN, M.C., M.A.
1963	REV. THOMAS FRASER, M.A.
1971	REV. DR. IAN MCINTOSH, M.A., TH.D., TH.M.
1994	REV. COLIN ANDERSON, B.A., B.D., S.T.M., M.PHIL.
2004	REV. PETER NIMMO, B.D., TH.M.

The Second Charge was established in c.1638 - 1640,

The Third Charge in 1704

APPENDIX 2
SOURCES AND REFERENCES

Much material was collected by word of mouth and varied documents, during my professional life as a chartered accountant in Inverness and as a member of the Old High Church. I am particularly indebted to the late Richard Milne FSAScot, sometime Inverness Burgh Librarian, and Clerk to the Congregational Board of the Old High, with whom I had many discussions when this project was a mere pipe-dream.

Unpublished work by Captain Douglas Wimberley, 1828 to 1912, Historian of Inverness and an Elder of the Parish Church, was a valuable source of information on pre-reformation history, in turn based in part on Invernessiana by Charles Fraser Mackintosh.

I am grateful to the Secretariat of the Queens Own Cameron Highlanders Regimental Association, and in particular Colonel Angus Fairrie, for making much useful information available to me.

Supplement of "The High Church and St. Stephen's", then of "The Old High Church and St Stephen's", 1921 to 1939.

The following list of titles, by no means exhaustive, may prove useful to anyone seeking further information.

The Old High Church, Inverness, booklet by the Rev F.J.L.Maclauchlan
Records of Inverness, Vols. 1 and 2
Inverness Kirk Session Records 1661 to 1800
Invernessiana, by Charles Fraser Mackintosh
Historic Inverness, by Gerald Pollitt
Inverness by James Millar
A History of Inverness by Murdoch Mackintosh
Inverness in the 18th Century by Leonella Longmore
The Northern Highlands, by James Barron
Memorabilia of Inverness by Donald Macdonald
The Hub of the Highlands, and many other publications by Inverness Field Club
Inverness local History and Archaeology, by Edward Meldrum
Proceedings of the Society of Antiquaries of Scotland
The Inverness Courier
Pevsner Architectural Guides